Reuben Sandwich cookbook

Discover the Art of Crafting Perfect Reuben Sandwiches with a Collection of Delicious Recipes

Jose Maria

Chapter Outline:

Introduction to the Reuben Legacy

- Origins and history of the Reuben sandwich
- Why the Reuben is a timeless classic

Mastering the Basics

- Anatomy of a classic Reuben
- Tips for selecting the best ingredients

The Perfect Corned Beef

- Homemade vs. store-bought
- Brining and cooking techniques

Sauerkraut Sensations

- Making sauerkraut from scratch
- Flavor variations

Russian Dressing Revelations

- Crafting the ideal Russian dressing
- Unique twists on the classic recipe

Swiss Cheese Varieties

- Exploring different Swiss cheeses
- Pairing cheese with other ingredients

Rye Bread Mastery

- Baking your own rye bread

- Choosing the right bread for your Reuben

Classic Reuben Recipe

- Step-by-step guide to the traditional Reuben sandwich
- Perfecting the layering technique

Variations on the Classic

- Turkey Reuben
- Vegetarian Reuben
- Seafood Reuben

Global Reuben Fusion

- Asian-inspired Reuben
- Mediterranean Reuben

Open-Faced Reubens

- Creative presentation ideas
- Exploring different toppings

Reuben-Inspired Salads

- Incorporating Reuben elements into salads
- Dressing variations

Reuben Wraps and Rolls

- Wrapping up the goodness
- Sushi-style Reuben rolls

The Reuben Burger Experience

- Turning the Reuben into a burger

- Unique burger toppings and condiments

Reuben Pizza Party

- Reuben-inspired pizza recipes
- Homemade pizza dough and sauce

Reuben Sides and Snacks

- Reuben sliders
- Reuben-stuffed mushrooms

Reuben Dips and Spreads

- Warm Reuben dip
- Reuben-inspired spreads for parties

Reuben Brunch Specials

- Breakfast Reuben recipes
- Reuben-inspired brunch cocktails

Healthy Reuben Alternatives

- Low-carb Reuben options
- Gluten-free variations

Dessert Delights with a Reuben Twist

- Reuben-inspired desserts
- Sweet treats for Reuben enthusiasts

Chapter 1: Introduction to the Reuben Legacy

Origins and History of the Reuben Sandwich

The Reuben sandwich, a celebrated classic in the world of comfort food, has a rich and flavorful history. Its origin story is woven with tales of culinary creativity, and its enduring popularity is a testament to its deliciousness.

The Birth of the Reuben:

The exact origins of the Reuben sandwich are the subject of some debate, but most agree that it emerged in the early 20th century. One popular theory attributes its creation to Arnold Reuben, a New York restaurateur. According to this tale, the sandwich was first crafted in the kitchen of Reuben's deli, a haven for those seeking hearty and satisfying meals.

Layers of Tradition:

The classic Reuben is a layered masterpiece, typically featuring corned beef, Swiss cheese, sauerkraut, and Russian dressing, all sandwiched between slices of rye bread. The balance of flavors and textures is what sets the Reuben apart—savory and salty corned beef, the tangy crunch of sauerkraut, the creaminess of Swiss cheese, and the zesty kick of Russian dressing.

Why the Reuben is a Timeless Classic
Versatility on a Plate:
What makes the Reuben truly timeless is its versatility. While the classic version remains an undisputed favorite, the Reuben has evolved over the years. From creative variations like the Turkey Reuben to international fusions such as the Asian-inspired Reuben, this sandwich has found its way into diverse culinary landscapes.

An Icon of Comfort:
Beyond its delightful taste, the Reuben holds a special place in the hearts of food enthusiasts as a symbol of comfort. Whether enjoyed at a deli, a diner, or homemade in your own kitchen, the Reuben has a unique ability to bring warmth and satisfaction with every bite.

In this cookbook, we embark on a journey to explore the art of crafting the perfect Reuben sandwich. From mastering the basics of its components to discovering innovative variations, get ready to elevate your Reuben game. Let's delve into the world of Reuben sandwiches and uncover the secrets behind this beloved culinary creation.

Chapter 2: Mastering the Basics

Anatomy of a Classic Reuben

Before you embark on your journey to create the perfect Reuben sandwich, it's essential to understand the key components that make this classic dish a true masterpiece.

1. Corned Beef:

The cornerstone of a classic Reuben is the succulent and flavorful corned beef. Whether you opt for store-bought or take on the challenge of preparing it at home, the corned beef should be tender, well-seasoned, and thinly sliced. Achieving the perfect texture is crucial for the overall enjoyment of your sandwich.

2. Swiss Cheese:

Swiss cheese brings a creamy and slightly nutty flavor to the Reuben. Opt for high-quality Swiss cheese and consider experimenting with different varieties. From traditional Emmental to Gruyere, the choice of cheese can add a unique twist to your Reuben experience.

3. Sauerkraut:

The tangy and crunchy sauerkraut is what gives the Reuben its signature kick. If you're feeling adventurous, try making your sauerkraut at home for an extra layer of freshness. When using store-bought sauerkraut, ensure it's well-drained to prevent your sandwich from becoming soggy.

4. Russian Dressing:

The secret sauce of the Reuben, Russian dressing provides a zesty and creamy counterbalance to the savory components. While you can find pre-made Russian dressing, crafting your own allows you to tailor the flavors to your liking. A harmonious blend of ketchup, mayonnaise, horseradish, and spices is the key to a perfect dressing.

5. Rye Bread:

Selecting the right rye bread is an art in itself. Look for a bread that is hearty enough to hold the robust fillings yet soft enough to provide a delightful bite. Dark or light rye seeded or plain—experiment with different varieties to find your preferred match.

Tips for Selecting the Best Ingredients

1. Quality Over Quantity:

Invest in high-quality ingredients. Whether it's the marbling of the corned beef, the freshness of sauerkraut, or the aged perfection of Swiss cheese, superior ingredients elevate the overall experience.

2. Freshness Matters:

opt for fresh ingredients whenever possible. Crisp sauerkraut, recently sliced corned beef, and just-baked rye bread contribute to a Reuben that bursts with flavor and texture.

3. Balance is Key:

Achieving the perfect Reuben is about balance. Ensure that no single element overpowers the others. The harmony of flavors—salty, tangy, creamy—is what makes the Reuben an enduring favorite.

4. Experiment with Varieties:

Don't be afraid to explore different varieties of corned beef, Swiss cheese, sauerkraut, and Russian dressing. The world of Reubens is vast, with room for creative interpretations and personal preferences.

Now that you understand the foundational elements of a classic Reuben sandwich and how to choose the best ingredients, you're ready to embark on the delicious journey of crafting your own Reuben masterpiece. In the following chapters, we'll delve deeper into each component, providing tips and recipes to hone your Reuben-making skills. Get ready to savor the satisfaction of a perfectly crafted Reuben sandwich!

Chapter 3: The Perfect Corned Beef

Homemade vs. Store-Bought

The choice between homemade and store-bought corned beef is a pivotal decision in your Reuben-making journey. Each option has its merits, and understanding the nuances will help you create a Reuben that suits your taste preferences.

1. Homemade Corned Beef:

Total Control:

Making corned beef from scratch grants you complete control over the quality and flavor. You can choose your cut of meat, tailor the brine to your liking, and experiment with additional spices to create a truly personalized experience.

Time and Patience:

Crafting homemade corned beef requires time and patience. The brining process can take several days, but the result is a corned beef that is uniquely yours, with flavors that develop over time.

2. Store-Bought Corned Beef:

Convenience:

Opting for store-bought corned beef is convenient, saving you the time and effort involved in the brining process. This is an excellent option for those who want to enjoy a Reuben without the extended preparation.

Varied Cuts:

Supermarkets offer a variety of corned beef cuts. Whether you prefer brisket or another cut, you can easily find pre-corned options that suit your taste.

Brining and Cooking Techniques

1. Brining Basics:

The Essential Ingredients:

A traditional corned beef brine typically includes salt, sugar, curing salt, and a blend of aromatic spices. Experiment with variations to find your preferred flavor profile.

The Importance of Time:

Allow the beef to soak in the brine for an optimal period. This not only imparts flavor but also ensures the characteristic pink hue associated with corned beef.

2. Cooking Methods:

Simmering on the Stovetop:

Simmering your corned beef on the stovetop is a classic method. The slow, gentle heat allows the meat to become tender while absorbing the flavors of the brine.

Oven-Baked Brilliance:

Baking your corned beef in the oven is an alternative method that can yield excellent results. This method is particularly convenient if you're preparing other components of your Reuben simultaneously.

3. Slow Cooker Convenience:

Set It and Forget It:

Using a slow cooker is a hassle-free way to cook corned beef. The low and slow approach results in exceptionally tender meat, and the set-it-and-forget-it convenience is perfect for busy schedules.

4. Experimentation is Key:

Flavor Infusions:

Don't be afraid to experiment with additional ingredients in your brine, such as garlic, bay leaves, or even a splash of your favorite beer. These subtle additions can elevate the overall flavor profile.

Smoking Adventures:

For those seeking a smoky twist, consider smoking your corned beef. This adds a layer of complexity to the flavor, making it a unique centerpiece for your Reuben.

Now armed with the knowledge of homemade versus store-bought corned beef and the various brining and cooking techniques, you're ready to take the next step in crafting the perfect Reuben sandwich. In the upcoming chapters, we'll explore the other components that contribute to the symphony of flavors in this iconic dish.

Chapter 4: Sauerkraut Sensations

Making Sauerkraut from Scratch

Sauerkraut, with its tangy and crunchy texture, is a cornerstone of the Reuben sandwich. Crafting your sauerkraut from scratch allows you to tailor the flavor and texture to perfection. In this chapter, we'll explore the art of making sauerkraut at home.

1. Selecting the Right Cabbage:

Choose fresh, firm cabbages for the best results. Green or red cabbage can both be used, each imparting its unique color and flavor to the sauerkraut.

2. Shredding and Salting:

Shred the cabbage finely, using a mandolin or a sharp knife. Sprinkle salt between the layers to draw out moisture. This process kickstarts the fermentation process.

3. Massaging and Packing:

Massage the cabbage to break down its cellular structure further. This encourages the release of liquid, creating the brine that aids fermentation. Pack the cabbage tightly into your fermentation vessel, ensuring it is submerged in its juices.

4. Fermentation Time:

Allow the sauerkraut to ferment at room temperature for optimal flavor development. The duration can vary but generally ranges from one to four weeks. Taste it periodically to find your preferred level of tanginess.

5. Storing Sauerkraut:

Once fermented, store your sauerkraut in the refrigerator. The cold temperature slows down the fermentation process, preserving the sauerkraut's crispness.

Flavor Variations

1. Classic Sauerkraut:

Stick to the traditional combination of cabbage and salt for a classic sauerkraut that complements the Reuben's other robust flavors.

2. Caraway and Juniper Berry Twist:

Add caraway seeds and juniper berries to the mix for a slightly spiced and aromatic sauerkraut. This variation brings an extra layer of complexity to your Reuben.

3. Spicy Red Sauerkraut:

Introduce heat by incorporating red chili flakes or thinly sliced hot peppers. The resulting spicy sauerkraut can add a fiery kick to your Reuben.

4. Apple and Fennel Fusion:

Experiment with sweetness by adding shredded apples and sliced fennel. This fruity and aromatic sauerkraut pairs exceptionally well with the savory elements of the Reuben.

5. Ginger and Turmeric Elevation:

Infuse your sauerkraut with grated ginger and turmeric for a zesty and anti-inflammatory twist. This variation adds a refreshing brightness to your Reuben.

As you embark on the journey of making sauerkraut from scratch and exploring flavor variations, remember that the art of sauerkraut-making is both a science and a culinary adventure. The unique sauerkraut you create will play a crucial role in the overall symphony of flavors in your Reuben sandwiches.

Chapter 5: Russian Dressing Revelations

Classic Reuben Sandwich Recipe
  Ingredients:

- 8 slices of quality rye bread
- 1 pound thinly sliced corned beef
- 1/2 pound Swiss cheese, thinly sliced
- 1 cup sauerkraut, well-drained
- Russian dressing (to taste)
- Butter for grilling

Instructions:
Prepare the Corned Beef:

1. If using store-bought corned beef, follow the package instructions for heating.

1. If using homemade corned beef, thinly slice it after cooking.

Build the Sandwich:

1. Lay out 8 slices of rye bread.

1. On 4 slices, layer the corned beef, Swiss cheese, and sauerkraut.

Russian Dressing Application:

1. Spread Russian dressing generously on the remaining 4 slices of bread.

Assembly:

1. Place the dressed slices on top of the corned beef, cheese, and sauerkraut slices, creating sandwiches.

Grilling:

1. Heat a griddle or a large skillet over medium heat.

1. Butter one side of each sandwich and place them on the griddle.

1. Grill until the bread is golden brown, and the cheese is melted, flipping halfway through.

Serve:

1. Remove from heat, slice diagonally, and serve immediately.

Enjoy your classic Reuben sandwich!

Homemade Sauerkraut Recipe

Ingredients:

- 1 medium-sized cabbage (green or red)
- 1 tablespoon salt (non-iodized)
- Caraway seeds (optional, for flavor)

Instructions:

Shred the Cabbage:

1. Remove outer leaves from the cabbage and cut it into quarters.

1. Thinly shred the cabbage using a knife or a mandolin.

Salt and Massage:

1. Sprinkle the shredded cabbage with salt as you layer it in a large

bowl.

1. Massage the cabbage with your hands for 5-10 minutes until it releases its juices.

Packing and Fermentation:

1. Pack the cabbage tightly into a fermentation vessel, ensuring it's submerged in its own juices.

1. If needed, add a little water to ensure the cabbage is fully submerged.

1. Add caraway seeds if desired.

Fermentation:

1. Cover the vessel with a clean cloth and secure it with a rubber band.

1. Allow it to ferment at room temperature for 1-4 weeks, tasting periodically until it reaches your desired tanginess.

Storage:

1. Once fermented, store the sauerkraut in the refrigerator to slow down the fermentation process.

Your homemade sauerkraut is now ready to be used in your Reuben sandwich!

Russian Dressing Recipe

Ingredients:

- 1/2 cup mayonnaise
- 2 tablespoons ketchup
- 1 tablespoon prepared horseradish
- 1 teaspoon Worcestershire sauce
- 2 tablespoons finely chopped dill pickles or dill pickle relish
- 1 teaspoon fresh lemon juice
- Pinch of paprika or cayenne pepper (optional)
- 1 clove garlic, minced (optional)
- Milk or buttermilk to adjust consistency
- Salt and pepper to taste

Instructions:

Mixing the Base:

In a bowl, whisk together mayonnaise and ketchup.

Adding Flavors:

Add horseradish, Worcestershire sauce, chopped pickles, lemon juice, and any optional ingredients (paprika, cayenne, garlic).

Adjusting Consistency:

Add milk or buttermilk gradually until you achieve the desired consistency.

Seasoning:

Season with salt and pepper to taste.

Storing:

Store the Russian dressing in the refrigerator until ready to use.

Your homemade Russian dressing is now ready to complement your Reuben sandwich!

Feel free to adjust these recipes based on your preferences, and enjoy the delightful process of creating a classic Reuben sandwich from scratch.

If you have any specific variations or modifications you'd like, let me know!

Chapter 6: Rye Bread Mastery

Baking Your Own Rye Bread

Rye bread, with its robust flavor and dense texture, is a crucial element in the art of crafting the perfect Reuben sandwich. In this chapter, we'll explore the satisfaction of baking your own rye bread from scratch.

Homemade Rye Bread Recipe

Ingredients:

- 2 cups dark rye flour
- 1 cup all-purpose flour
- 1 packet (2 1/4 teaspoons) active dry yeast
- 1 1/4 cups warm water (around 110°F/43°C)
- 2 tablespoons molasses
- 1 tablespoon caraway seeds (optional)
- 1 teaspoon salt
- 1 tablespoon vegetable oil

Instructions:

Activate the Yeast:

In a small bowl, combine the warm water and molasses. Sprinkle the yeast over the mixture, stir gently, and let it sit for about 5-10 minutes until it becomes frothy.

Mixing the Dough:

1. In a large mixing bowl, combine the dark rye flour, all-purpose flour, caraway seeds (if using), and salt.

1. Make a well in the center and pour in the yeast mixture.

1. Gradually incorporate the flour into the liquid until a dough forms.

Kneading:
Turn the dough out onto a floured surface and knead for about 8-10 minutes until it becomes smooth and elastic.

First Rise:
Place the dough in a greased bowl, cover it with a damp cloth, and let it rise in a warm place for 1-1.5 hours or until it doubles in size.

Shaping:
Punch down the dough and shape it into a round or oval loaf.

Second Rise:

1. Place the shaped dough on a baking sheet, cover it, and let it rise for another 30-45 minutes.

Preheat and Bake:

1. Preheat your oven to 375°F (190°C).

1. Before baking, brush the top of the loaf with vegetable oil to achieve a glossy finish.

1. Bake for 25-30 minutes or until the bread sounds hollow when tapped on the bottom.

Cooling:

1. Allow the rye bread to cool completely on a wire rack before slicing.

Now you have a homemade rye bread ready to serve as the canvas for your Reuben masterpiece!

Choosing the Right Bread for Your Reuben

When selecting or making rye bread for your Reuben, consider the following:

Dark or Light Rye:

Dark rye bread, with its higher percentage of rye flour, has a stronger flavor. Light rye, which incorporates more wheat flour, is milder. Choose based on your preference and the flavor profile you desire for your Reuben.

Texture:

A denser rye bread stands up well to the substantial fillings of a Reuben. Look for a bread with a hearty texture that won't get soggy when layered with sauerkraut and Russian dressing.

Seeds or Plain:

Caraway seeds are a classic addition to rye bread and can enhance the overall experience of a Reuben. However, a plain rye bread can also be an excellent choice, allowing the other flavors to shine.

Freshness:

Whether you buy or bake your rye bread, freshness is key. A slightly crisp crust and soft interior make for the ideal Reuben experience.

Now armed with the mastery of baking your own rye bread and insights into choosing the right bread for your Reuben, you're ready to assemble a sandwich that not only tastes extraordinary but also boasts a homemade touch from start to finish.

Chapter 7: Classic Reuben Recipe

Crafting the perfect Reuben sandwich involves a delicate balance of flavors, textures, and precise layering. In this chapter, we'll provide a step-by-step guide to the traditional Reuben and delve into the art of perfecting the layering technique.

Ingredients:

- 8 slices of rye bread
- 1 pound thinly sliced corned beef
- 1/2 pound Swiss cheese, thinly sliced
- 1 cup sauerkraut, well-drained
- Russian dressing (to taste)
- Butter for grilling

Step-by-Step Guide:

1. Gather Your Ingredients:

Ensure you have all the components ready: thinly sliced corned beef, Swiss cheese, well-drained sauerkraut, Russian dressing, and slices of rye bread.

2. Preheat the Griddle or Skillet:

Heat a griddle or a large skillet over medium heat.

3. Butter the Bread:

Butter one side of each slice of rye bread. This will contribute to a golden-brown, crispy exterior.

4. Build the Foundation:

Place four slices of rye bread, buttered side down, on your work surface.

5. Layer the Corned Beef:

Add a generous portion of thinly sliced corned beef on each slice of bread.

6. Add Swiss Cheese:

Layer Swiss cheese over the corned beef. The cheese will melt during grilling, contributing to the sandwich's creamy texture.

7. Pile on the Sauerkraut:

Spoon sauerkraut evenly onto each sandwich. Ensure it's well-drained to prevent sogginess.

8. Drizzle with Russian Dressing:

Spread Russian dressing on the non-buttered side of the remaining four slices of rye bread.

9. Create the Top Layer:

Place the dressed slices, Russian dressing side down, on top of the sauerkraut. You've now created the Reuben sandwiches.

10. Grill to Perfection:

Place the sandwiches on the preheated griddle or skillet.

Grill until the bread becomes golden brown, and the cheese is melted, usually 3-4 minutes per side.

11. Check for Crispiness:

Press the sandwich with a spatula to ensure the bread is crisp, and the fillings are heated through.

12. Slice and Serve:

Remove the Reuben sandwiches from the griddle.

Slice each sandwich diagonally for an elegant presentation.

13. Enjoy Immediately:

Reubens are best enjoyed fresh off the griddle when the bread is crispy, and the fillings are warm and gooey.

Perfecting the Layering Technique:

1. Start with a Sturdy Foundation:

Begin with a base of hearty rye bread, ensuring it can support the substantial fillings without becoming soggy.

2. Evenly Distribute Corned Beef:

Layer the thinly sliced corned beef evenly to ensure each bite has a savory, meaty goodness.

3. Swiss Cheese for Creaminess:

Add Swiss cheese over the corned beef, allowing it to melt and create a lusciously creamy texture.

4. Sauerkraut Spread:

Spoon sauerkraut evenly across the sandwich, ensuring it's well-drained to maintain the sandwich's crispness.

5. Russian Dressing Binding:

The Russian dressing serves as a flavorful binding agent. Spread it on the bread to infuse the entire sandwich with its zesty goodness.

6. Balance is Key:

Maintain a balance of ingredients in each layer. Avoid overwhelming one flavor, ensuring a harmonious blend with every bite.

7. Grill to Crispy Perfection:

Grilling the Reuben not only heats the fillings but also imparts a delightful crispiness to the bread.

8. Diagonal Slicing for Elegance:

Slicing the Reuben diagonally not only makes for an elegant presentation but also ensures easy handling and reveals the layers within.

Now that you've mastered the step-by-step guide and perfected the layering technique, you're ready to savor the classic Reuben experience.

Chapter 8: Variations on the Classic Reuben

While the classic Reuben holds a special place in culinary tradition, exploring variations allows for diverse and delightful experiences. In this chapter, we'll explore three exciting variations: the Turkey Reuben, the Vegetarian Reuben, and the Seafood Reuben.

Turkey Reuben

Ingredients:

- Sliced turkey (smoked or roasted)
- Swiss cheese, thinly sliced
- Coleslaw (homemade or store-bought)
- Russian dressing
- Rye bread

Instructions:

Assemble the Base:

Lay out slices of rye bread.

Layer the Turkey:

Place generous portions of sliced turkey on each slice of bread.

Add Swiss Cheese:

Layer Swiss cheese over the turkey. The mild flavor complements the turkey beautifully.

Top with Coleslaw:

Add a refreshing twist by incorporating coleslaw. Its crunch and tangy flavors enhance the turkey Reuben.

Drizzle with Russian Dressing:

Spread Russian dressing on the other side of the bread slices.

Grill to Perfection:

Grill the sandwich until the bread is golden brown, and the cheese is melted.

Slice and Serve:

Diagonally slice the Turkey Reuben for a visually appealing presentation.

Vegetarian Reuben
Ingredients:

- Grilled or marinated portobello mushrooms
- Swiss cheese, thinly sliced
- Sauerkraut
- Russian dressing
- Rye bread

Instructions:
Prepare the Portobello Mushrooms:
Grill or marinate portobello mushrooms for a savory, meaty flavor.
Assemble the Sandwich:
Lay out slices of rye bread.
Layer the Mushrooms:
Place the grilled or marinated portobello mushrooms on each slice of bread.

Add Swiss Cheese:
Layer Swiss cheese over the mushrooms. The cheese adds a creamy element to the vegetarian Reuben.
Top with Sauerkraut:
Add sauerkraut for a tangy kick, providing balance to the umami of the mushrooms.
Drizzle with Russian Dressing:
Spread Russian dressing on the other side of the bread slices.
Grill to Perfection:
Grill the sandwich until the bread is golden brown, and the cheese is melted.
Slice and Serve:
Diagonally slice the Vegetarian Reuben for an enticing presentation.

Seafood Reuben
Ingredients:

- Grilled or pan-seared fish fillets (such as cod or tilapia)
- Swiss cheese, thinly sliced
- Coleslaw with a citrus dressing
- Tartar sauce
- Rye bread

Instructions:
Prepare the Fish Fillets:
Grill or pan-sear fish fillets until they are cooked through and have a golden crust.
Assemble the Sandwich:
Lay out slices of rye bread.
Layer the Fish Fillets:
Place the grilled or pan-seared fish fillets on each slice of bread.

Add Swiss Cheese:
Layer Swiss cheese over the fish. The mildness of Swiss cheese complements the delicate flavor of the fish.
Top with Coleslaw:
Add coleslaw with a citrus dressing for a refreshing contrast to the seafood.
Drizzle with Tartar Sauce:
Instead of Russian dressing, drizzle tartar sauce on the other side of the bread slices.
Grill to Perfection:
Grill the sandwich until the bread is golden brown, and the cheese is melted.
Slice and Serve:

Diagonally slice the Seafood Reuben for a visually appealing presentation.

These variations on the classic Reuben allow for diverse culinary experiences, catering to different tastes and dietary preferences. Feel free to customize these recipes further based on your preferences or get creative with your own variations!

Chapter 9: Global Reuben Fusion

Bringing the Reuben sandwich into the realm of global flavors opens up exciting possibilities. In this chapter, we'll explore two unique fusions: the Asian-inspired Reuben and the Mediterranean Reuben.

Asian-Inspired Reuben

Ingredients:

- Sliced teriyaki-marinated chicken or tofu
- Gouda or provolone cheese, thinly sliced
- Kimchi (store-bought or homemade)
- Sriracha mayo
- Sesame seed-coated bread (rye or white)

Instructions:

Marinate the Chicken or Tofu:

Marinate chicken or tofu in a teriyaki sauce for a savory and slightly sweet flavor.

Assemble the Sandwich:

Lay out slices of sesame seed-coated bread.

Layer the Marinated Chicken or Tofu:

Place the teriyaki-marinated chicken or tofu on each slice of bread.

Add Gouda or Provolone Cheese:

Layer Gouda or provolone cheese over the marinated protein. These cheeses complement the Asian-inspired flavors.

Top with Kimchi:

Add a generous portion of kimchi for a spicy and tangy kick.

Drizzle with Sriracha Mayo:

Drizzle Sriracha mayo on the other side of the bread slices for an extra layer of heat.

Grill to Perfection:

Grill the sandwich until the bread is toasted, and the cheese is melted.

Slice and Serve:

Diagonally slice the Asian-Inspired Reuben for a modern and flavorful twist.

Mediterranean Reuben

Ingredients:

- Sliced grilled chicken or falafel
- Feta cheese, crumbled
- Tzatziki sauce
- Roasted red peppers, sliced
- Olive tapenade
- Whole grain bread

Instructions:

Prepare the Protein:

Grill chicken or prepare falafel, ensuring they are seasoned with Mediterranean spices.

Assemble the Sandwich:

Lay out slices of whole grain bread.

Layer the Grilled Chicken or Falafel:

Place the grilled chicken or falafel on each slice of bread.

Add Feta Cheese:

Sprinkle crumbled feta cheese over the protein. The briny flavor of feta complements Mediterranean cuisine.

Top with Roasted Red Peppers:

Layer slices of roasted red peppers for a sweet and smoky flavor.

Spread Tzatziki Sauce:

Spread a generous amount of tzatziki sauce on the other side of the bread slices.

Add Olive Tapenade:

Enhance the Mediterranean flavors by adding a spoonful of olive tapenade.

Grill to Perfection:

Grill the sandwich until the bread is crispy, and the fillings are warmed.

Slice and Serve:

Diagonally slice the Mediterranean Reuben for a sophisticated and flavorful experience.

These global Reuben fusions showcase the adaptability and versatility of this classic sandwich. Feel free to experiment with these recipes and incorporate your favorite global flavors for a personalized twist on the Reuben!

Chapter 10: Open-Faced Reubens

Embracing the open-faced concept with Reubens provides an opportunity for creative presentations and allows for a more indulgent experience. In this chapter, we'll explore creative presentation ideas and suggest different toppings to elevate the open-faced Reuben.

Creative Presentation Ideas:

1. Stacked Tower:

Assemble the Reuben components in a vertical stack, allowing each layer to showcase its distinct flavors. This creates a visually striking presentation.

2. Deconstructed Style:

Arrange each component of the Reuben separately on the plate, allowing diners to build their bites. This style provides an interactive dining experience.

3. Circular Arrangement:

Place the open-faced Reuben components in a circular pattern, allowing the eye to follow the layers. This presentation creates a sense of balance and harmony.

4. Artistic Drizzles:

Use Russian dressing or other sauces to create artistic drizzles on the plate. This not only adds flavor but also enhances the visual appeal.

5. Garnish Galore:

Garnish the open-faced Reuben with fresh herbs, microgreens, or edible flowers for a touch of elegance and freshness.

6. Colorful Contrasts:

Introduce colorful elements like cherry tomatoes or pickled red onions to add vibrancy and contrast to the presentation.

Exploring Different Toppings:

1. Pickled Red Onions:

The tanginess of pickled red onions adds a burst of flavor and a pop of color to the open-faced Reuben.

2. Microgreens:

Top the Reuben with delicate microgreens for a subtle, fresh flavor and an elegant appearance.

3. Crispy Bacon Bits:

Sprinkle crispy bacon bits on top for an extra layer of crunch and a smoky undertone.

4. Avocado Slices:

Add creamy avocado slices to bring a buttery texture and richness to the open-faced Reuben.

5. Poached Egg:

Place a perfectly poached egg on top for a luxurious and indulgent twist, creating a Reuben Benedict.

6. Dijon Mustard Drizzle:

Drizzle Dijon mustard on the open-faced Reuben for a sharp and tangy kick that complements the other flavors.

7. Pomegranate Seeds:

Sprinkle vibrant pomegranate seeds on top for a burst of sweetness and a delightful crunch.

8. Caramelized Onions:

Add a layer of sweet and savory caramelized onions for depth of flavor.

9. Zesty Radish Slices:

Incorporate thin slices of zesty radishes for a refreshing and peppery element.

10. Chopped Fresh Dill:

Garnish with chopped fresh dill to add a burst of herbaceous freshness.

Experimenting with different toppings not only enhances the flavor profile of the open-faced Reuben but also allows for personalization based on individual preferences. Combine these topping ideas with creative presentation styles to elevate your open-faced Reuben experience.

Chapter 11: Reuben-Inspired Salads

Introducing Reuben-inspired elements into salads offers a refreshing and lighter take on the classic flavors. In this chapter, we'll explore how to incorporate Reuben components into salads and provide variations for dressings that complement these vibrant dishes.

Incorporating Reuben Elements into Salads:

1. Corned Beef Croutons:

Thinly slice leftover corned beef into bite-sized pieces, pan-fry until crispy, and use them as a flavorful alternative to croutons.

2. Swiss Cheese Cubes:

Cube Swiss cheese and scatter it throughout the salad for a creamy and savory element.

3. Sauerkraut Crunch:

Add a generous spoonful of well-drained sauerkraut for a tangy and crunchy kick.

4. Rye Bread Crisps:

Toast thin slices of rye bread until crisp, break them into pieces, and use them as crunchy croutons in the salad.

5. Russian Dressing Drizzle:

Drizzle a light amount of Russian dressing over the salad as a zesty and flavorful dressing.

6. Pickled Vegetables:

Introduce pickled vegetables such as cucumbers or radishes to add a refreshing and tangy element.

7. Horseradish Kick:

Incorporate a horseradish-infused dressing to impart a bold and spicy kick to the salad.

8. Dill Garnish:

Garnish the salad with fresh dill for a burst of herbaceous freshness.

9. Avocado Creaminess:

Include slices of creamy avocado to balance the acidity of sauerkraut and add a buttery texture.

10. Grilled Chicken Strips:

Grill chicken strips with Reuben-inspired seasonings and place them atop the salad for a protein-packed variation.

Dressing Variations:

1. Russian Yogurt Dressing:

Mix Russian dressing with Greek yogurt for a lighter and tangy dressing option.

2. Horseradish Ranch Dressing:

Blend ranch dressing with a hint of horseradish for a creamy and mildly spicy dressing.

3. Thousand Island Vinaigrette:

Transform classic Thousand Island dressing into a vinaigrette by adding a splash of balsamic vinegar for a tangy twist.

4. Lemon-Herb Dressing:

Whisk together fresh lemon juice, olive oil, chopped dill, and a touch of honey for a vibrant and herbaceous dressing.

5. Mustard-Maple Vinaigrette:

Combine Dijon mustard, maple syrup, and apple cider vinegar for a sweet and tangy vinaigrette.

6. Cider-Horseradish Dressing:

Mix apple cider vinegar with horseradish for a refreshing and bold dressing that complements the Reuben elements.

7. Creamy Avocado Dressing:

Blend ripe avocado with lime juice, Greek yogurt, and garlic for a creamy and avocado-infused dressing.

8. Sauerkraut Citrus Dressing:

Create a unique dressing by blending sauerkraut with orange or grapefruit juice for a zesty and probiotic-rich option.

9. Garlic-Pickle Aioli:

Mix minced garlic and finely chopped dill pickles into mayonnaise for a garlicky and pickle-infused aioli.

10. Caramelized Onion Balsamic Glaze:

Caramelize onions and blend them with balsamic vinegar for a sweet and savory glaze that enhances the salad.

These Reuben-inspired salads and dressing variations provide a fresh and inventive way to enjoy the classic flavors in a lighter format. Whether you prefer a classic Reuben salad or want to explore new combinations, these ideas offer a delicious and nutritious twist.

Chapter 12: Reuben Wraps and Rolls

Transforming the classic Reuben into wraps and rolls brings a playful and portable twist to this iconic dish. In this chapter, we'll explore different ways to wrap up the goodness, including a sushi-style Reuben roll that combines the best of both worlds.

Wrapping Up the Goodness:

1. Classic Reuben Wrap:

Ingredients:

- Large tortillas
- Thinly sliced corned beef
- Swiss cheese
- Sauerkraut
- Russian dressing

Instructions:

1. Lay out a tortilla.
2. Layer corned beef, Swiss cheese, sauerkraut, and Russian dressing.
3. Wrap tightly, slice in half, and secure with toothpicks if needed.

2. Rye Bread Pinwheels:

Ingredients:

- Sliced rye bread
- Cream cheese
- Pastrami or corned beef
- Sauerkraut
- Mustard

Instructions:

1. Spread cream cheese on rye bread slices.
2. Layer with pastrami or corned beef, sauerkraut, and a drizzle of mustard.
3. Roll up tightly, slice into pinwheels, and secure with toothpicks.

3. Reuben Lettuce Wraps:
Ingredients:

- Large lettuce leaves (such as iceberg or butter lettuce)
- Thinly sliced corned beef
- Swiss cheese
- Sauerkraut
- Russian dressing

Instructions:

1. Place a few slices of corned beef on a lettuce leaf.
2. Add Swiss cheese, sauerkraut, and a drizzle of Russian dressing.
3. Wrap the lettuce around the fillings, securing with a toothpick.

4. Grilled Reuben Burritos:
Ingredients:

- Large flour tortillas
- Grilled corned beef slices
- Melted Swiss cheese
- Sauerkraut
- Russian dressing

Instructions:

1. Lay out a tortilla.
2. Place grilled corned beef slices, melted Swiss cheese, sauerkraut, and Russian dressing.
3. Roll into a burrito, slice in half, and serve.

Sushi-Style Reuben Rolls:
Ingredients:

- Sushi nori sheets
- Sushi rice
- Corned beef slices
- Swiss cheese, thinly sliced
- Sauerkraut
- Russian dressing
- Soy sauce for dipping (optional)

Instructions:
Prepare Sushi Rice:

1. Cook sushi rice according to package instructions and let it cool to room temperature.

Assemble the Ingredients:

1. Lay a sushi nori sheet on a bamboo sushi rolling mat.
2. Spread a thin layer of sushi rice over the nori, leaving a small border at the top.

Layer the Fillings:

1. Arrange corned beef slices, Swiss cheese, sauerkraut, and a drizzle of Russian dressing along the center of the rice.

Rolling Technique:

1. Carefully lift the bamboo mat's edge closest to you and start rolling away from you, tucking the ingredients in as you go.

Seal the Edge:

1. Moisten the nori's border with a bit of water to seal the edge of the roll.

Slice and Serve:

1. Use a sharp, damp knife to slice the roll into bite-sized pieces.

Optional: Serve with Soy Sauce:

1. If desired, serve the sushi-style Reuben rolls with a side of soy sauce for dipping.

These Reuben wraps and rolls provide a convenient and fun way to enjoy the classic flavors in a different format. The sushi-style Reuben roll, in particular, offers a unique fusion of the traditional Reuben and sushi, creating a delightful and unexpected culinary experience.

Chapter 13: The Reuben Burger Experience

Turning the classic Reuben into a burger is a bold and flavorful move that combines the best of two beloved dishes. In this chapter, we'll explore the steps to create a Reuben-inspired burger and suggest unique toppings and condiments to elevate the burger experience.

Creating the Reuben Burger:

Ingredients:

- Ground beef patties (or your choice of protein)
- Rye burger buns
- Swiss cheese slices
- Thinly sliced corned beef
- Sauerkraut
- Russian dressing
- Butter for toasting buns

Instructions:

Grill the Patties:

1. Season the ground beef patties with salt and pepper.
2. Grill the patties to your desired level of doneness.

Toast the Rye Buns:

1. While the patties are grilling, lightly butter and toast the rye burger buns until golden brown.

Melt Swiss Cheese:

1. In the last minute of grilling, place a slice of Swiss cheese on each patty to melt.

Layer Corned Beef:

1. Place a generous layer of thinly sliced corned beef on the bottom half of each toasted bun.

Add the Patty:

1. Place a grilled patty with melted Swiss cheese on top of the corned beef layer.

Top with Sauerkraut:

1. Pile sauerkraut on top of the Swiss cheese-covered patty.

Drizzle with Russian Dressing:

1. Drizzle Russian dressing over the sauerkraut, and place the top half of the toasted bun to complete the burger.

Secure with Toothpicks:

1. Insert toothpicks through the center to secure the burger layers, making it easier to handle.

Now you have a Reuben-inspired burger ready to be enjoyed! The combination of the juicy patty, melted Swiss cheese, savory corned beef, tangy sauerkraut, and zesty Russian dressing creates a burger experience like no other.

Unique Burger Toppings and Condiments:

1. Pickled Mustard Seeds:

Add a burst of tangy flavor by incorporating pickled mustard seeds.

2. Crispy Pastrami Chips:

Replace traditional bacon with crispy pastrami chips for an extra layer of crunch and flavor.

3. Horseradish Aioli:

Mix horseradish into aioli for a creamy and spicy condiment.

4. Caramelized Onion Jam:

Elevate the sweetness by adding caramelized onion jam to the burger.

5. Dill Pickle Relish:

Create a zesty relish by finely chopping dill pickles and mixing them with a touch of vinegar.

6. Spicy Russian Sauce:

Infuse Russian dressing with hot sauce for a spicy twist.

7. Fried Egg Topping:

Amp up the indulgence by adding a fried egg on top of the burger for a rich and gooey element.

8. Watercress or Arugula:

opt for peppery greens like watercress or arugula for a fresh and vibrant addition.

9. Crispy Swiss Cheese Tuiles:

Create crispy Swiss cheese tuiles by baking slices until golden brown and using them as a crunchy topping.

10. Balsamic Onion Marmalade:

Slow-cook onions with balsamic vinegar to create a sweet and tangy onion marmalade.

Experimenting with these unique toppings and condiments allows you to personalize your Reuben burger and create a culinary masterpiece that reflects your taste preferences. In the upcoming chapters, we'll explore Reuben-inspired sides, beverages, and even desserts for a complete and satisfying culinary journey.

Chapter 14: Reuben Pizza Party

Transforming the classic Reuben into a pizza is a delicious and creative way to enjoy these flavors in a new form. In this chapter, we'll explore Reuben-inspired pizza recipes and guide you through making homemade pizza dough and sauce.

Homemade Pizza Dough:

Ingredients:

- 3 1/2 to 4 cups all-purpose flour
- 1 teaspoon sugar
- 1 packet (2 1/4 teaspoons) active dry yeast
- 1 1/2 teaspoons salt
- 1 1/2 cups warm water (110°F/43°C)
- 2 tablespoons olive oil

Instructions:

Activate the Yeast:

In a bowl, combine warm water and sugar. Sprinkle yeast over the water and let it sit for 5-10 minutes until it becomes foamy.

Mix the Dough:

In a large mixing bowl, combine 3 1/2 cups of flour and salt. Make a well in the center and pour in the yeast mixture and olive oil.

Knead the Dough:

- Mix until a dough forms, then transfer it to a floured surface.
- Knead the dough for about 8-10 minutes until it becomes smooth and elastic. If it's too sticky, add more flour a little at a time.

First Rise:

Place the dough in a lightly oiled bowl, cover it with a damp cloth, and let it rise in a warm place for 1-2 hours or until it doubles in size.

Punch Down and Second Rise:

Punch down the dough, then let it rise again for about 30 minutes.

Preheat Oven:

Preheat your oven to the highest setting (usually around 475°F/ 245°C).

Roll Out and Shape:

Roll out the dough on a floured surface to your desired thickness and shape.

Homemade Pizza Sauce:

Ingredients:

- 1 can (14 ounces) crushed tomatoes
- 2 cloves garlic, minced
- 1 teaspoon dried oregano
- 1 teaspoon dried basil
- Salt and pepper to taste
- 1 tablespoon olive oil

Instructions:

Sauté Garlic:

In a saucepan, heat olive oil over medium heat. Add minced garlic and sauté until fragrant.

Add Tomatoes and Herbs:

Pour in the crushed tomatoes, oregano, basil, salt, and pepper. Stir well.

Simmer:

Allow the sauce to simmer for about 15-20 minutes, stirring occasionally. Taste and adjust seasoning if needed.

Cool:

Let the sauce cool before spreading it on the pizza dough.

Reuben Pizza Recipe:

Ingredients:

- Homemade pizza dough
- Homemade pizza sauce
- Thinly sliced corned beef
- Swiss cheese, shredded
- Sauerkraut, drained
- Russian dressing

Instructions:
Preheat Oven:
Preheat your oven to 475°F (245°C).
Roll Out the Dough:
Roll out the homemade pizza dough on a floured surface to your preferred thickness.
Assemble the Pizza:

- Spread a layer of homemade pizza sauce over the dough.
- Add a generous amount of shredded Swiss cheese.
- Arrange thinly sliced corned beef evenly on top.
- Spoon sauerkraut over the pizza.

Bake:

- Carefully transfer the assembled pizza to a preheated pizza stone or baking sheet.
- Bake in the preheated oven for 12-15 minutes or until the crust is golden and the cheese is melted and bubbly.

Finish and Drizzle:
Once out of the oven, drizzle with Russian dressing for that Reuben flavor.
Slice and Serve:
Allow the pizza to cool for a few minutes before slicing.
Enjoy your Reuben-inspired pizza creation! The combination of the crispy crust, savory corned beef, melted Swiss cheese, tangy sauerkraut,

and zesty Russian dressing will make this pizza a favorite at your next pizza party.

Chapter 15: Reuben Sides and Snacks

Complementing the main Reuben dishes with sides and snacks that carry the same delicious flavors ensures a well-rounded and satisfying culinary experience. In this chapter, we'll explore two delightful Reuben-inspired offerings: Reuben sliders and Reuben-stuffed mushrooms.

Reuben Sliders:
Ingredients:

- Slider buns
- Thinly sliced corned beef
- Swiss cheese, sliced
- Sauerkraut
- Russian dressing
- Butter, for toasting

Instructions:
Preheat and Slice:

- Preheat your oven to 350°F (175°C).
- Slice slider buns horizontally.

Layer the Ingredients:
On the bottom half of each slider bun, layer thinly sliced corned beef, Swiss cheese, and sauerkraut.
Dress with Russian Dressing:
Drizzle a spoonful of Russian dressing over the sauerkraut.
Top and Toast:

- Place the top half of the slider bun on the dressed ingredients.

- Lightly butter the tops of the sliders.

Bake:
Arrange the sliders on a baking sheet and bake in the preheated oven for about 10 minutes, or until the cheese is melted, and the sliders are warmed through.
Serve:
Serve these Reuben sliders warm and enjoy the delightful combination of flavors.

Reuben-Stuffed Mushrooms:
Ingredients:

- Large mushroom caps
- Cream cheese
- Thinly sliced corned beef, finely chopped
- Sauerkraut, drained and squeezed
- Swiss cheese, shredded
- Russian dressing
- Fresh parsley, chopped (for garnish)

Instructions:
Prepare Mushrooms:
Clean and remove stems from large mushroom caps, creating a hollow space for stuffing.
Prepare Filling:
In a bowl, mix cream cheese, finely chopped corned beef, drained sauerkraut, and shredded Swiss cheese until well combined.

Stuff the Mushrooms:
Spoon the filling into each mushroom cap, packing it in tightly.

Bake:

Place the stuffed mushrooms on a baking sheet and bake in a preheated oven at 375°F (190°C) for about 15-20 minutes or until the mushrooms are cooked and the filling is heated through.

Drizzle with Dressing:

Once out of the oven, drizzle each stuffed mushroom with a bit of Russian dressing.

Garnish and Serve:

Garnish with chopped fresh parsley and serve these Reuben-stuffed mushrooms as a delightful appetizer or side.

These Reuben sliders and Reuben-stuffed mushrooms offer bite-sized versions of the classic flavors, making them perfect for gatherings, parties, or simply as tasty snacks. In the upcoming chapters, we'll explore Reuben-inspired beverages and even desserts to complete your culinary journey.

Chapter 16: Reuben Dips and Spreads

Dips and spreads are perfect for social gatherings, and when they're Reuben-inspired, you're guaranteed to have a crowd-pleaser. In this chapter, we'll explore a Warm Reuben Dip and Reuben-inspired spreads that are sure to be the highlight of your next party.

Warm Reuben Dip:

Ingredients:

- 8 oz cream cheese, softened
- 1 cup shredded Swiss cheese
- 1 cup chopped corned beef
- 1 cup sauerkraut, drained and squeezed
- 1/2 cup mayonnaise
- 1/4 cup Russian dressing
- 1 cup shredded mozzarella cheese (for topping)
- Rye crackers or bread for dipping

Instructions:

Preheat Oven:

Preheat your oven to 375°F (190°C).

Combine Ingredients:

In a mixing bowl, combine softened cream cheese, shredded Swiss cheese, chopped corned beef, drained sauerkraut, mayonnaise, and Russian dressing. Mix until well combined.

Transfer to Baking Dish:

Transfer the mixture to a baking dish, spreading it evenly.

Top with Mozzarella:

Sprinkle shredded mozzarella cheese on top of the mixture.

Bake:

Bake in the preheated oven for 20-25 minutes or until the dip is hot and bubbly, and the cheese is melted and golden brown.

Serve:

Allow the dip to cool slightly before serving. Serve with rye crackers or bread for dipping.

This Warm Reuben Dip captures all the classic flavors of a Reuben sandwich in a gooey, savory dip that's perfect for entertaining.

Reuben-Inspired Spreads for Parties:

1. Russian Reuben Spread:

Mix Russian dressing with cream cheese for a tangy and creamy spread.

2. Sauerkraut and Swiss Dip:

Combine finely chopped sauerkraut with shredded Swiss cheese and mayonnaise for a simple yet flavorful spread.

3. Corned Beef Pâté:

Blend chopped corned beef with cream cheese, Dijon mustard, and a touch of Worcestershire sauce for a rich and savory pâté.

4. Dill Pickle Relish Spread:

Mix dill pickle relish with cream cheese for a spread with a zesty and crunchy kick.

5. Horseradish Infusion:

Infuse cream cheese with horseradish for a spread that adds a bold and spicy element.

6. Swiss and Onion Delight:

Combine shredded Swiss cheese with caramelized onions and mayonnaise for a spread that's both sweet and savory.

7. Thousand Island Cream:

Blend Thousand Island dressing with softened cream cheese for a creamy and tangy spread.

8. Bacon and Chive Reuben Butter:

Mix crispy bacon bits and chopped chives into softened butter for a flavorful and indulgent spread.

9. Pickle and Mustard Harmony:

Combine finely chopped dill pickles with Dijon mustard and cream cheese for a spread with a balanced tangy and savory profile.

10. Garlic Herb Reuben Dip:

Blend cream cheese with minced garlic, fresh herbs (such as parsley and chives), and a squeeze of lemon for a refreshing and aromatic spread.

These Reuben-inspired spreads offer a variety of flavors and textures that can be paired with crackers, bread, or vegetables for a delightful party experience.

Chapter 17: Reuben Brunch Specials

Brunch is a wonderful time to enjoy the comforting flavors of a Reuben in unique and delicious ways. In this chapter, we'll explore Breakfast Reuben recipes and Reuben-inspired brunch cocktails that are perfect for a leisurely weekend brunch.

Breakfast Reuben Recipes:

1. Reuben Benedict:

Ingredients:

- English muffins
- Poached eggs
- Corned beef slices
- Hollandaise sauce
- Chopped chives (for garnish)

Instructions:

1. Toast English muffins and place slices of corned beef on each half.
2. Top with a poached egg and generously drizzle with hollandaise sauce.
3. Garnish with chopped chives.

2. Reuben Omelet:

Ingredients:

- Eggs
- Thinly sliced corned beef
- Swiss cheese, shredded
- Sauerkraut

- Russian dressing
- Chopped fresh parsley (for garnish)

Instructions:

1. Whisk eggs and pour into a heated and greased skillet.
2. Add corned beef, sauerkraut, and Swiss cheese to one side of the omelet.
3. Fold the omelet in half and cook until eggs are set.
4. Drizzle with Russian dressing and garnish with chopped parsley.

3. Reuben Breakfast Burrito:

Ingredients:

- Large flour tortillas
- Scrambled eggs
- Thinly sliced corned beef
- Swiss cheese, shredded
- Sauerkraut
- Russian dressing

Instructions:

1. Lay out a tortilla and fill it with scrambled eggs, corned beef, Swiss cheese, sauerkraut, and a drizzle of Russian dressing.
2. Roll into a burrito and serve.

4. Rye Pancakes with Reuben Toppings:

Ingredients:

- Rye pancake batter
- Thinly sliced corned beef
- Swiss cheese, shredded

- Sauerkraut
- Russian dressing

Instructions:

1. Prepare rye pancake batter and cook pancakes.
2. Top each pancake with corned beef, Swiss cheese, sauerkraut, and a drizzle of Russian dressing.

Reuben-Inspired Brunch Cocktails:
1. Bloody Mary Reuben Twist:
Ingredients:

- 1 1/2 oz vodka
- 3 oz tomato juice
- 1/2 oz lemon juice
- 1 dash Worcestershire sauce
- Celery salt and black pepper
- Garnishes: Pickle spear, cherry tomatoes, mini Reuben skewers

Instructions:

1. Rim a glass with celery salt and black pepper.
2. Fill the glass with ice.
3. In a shaker, combine vodka, tomato juice, lemon juice, and Worcestershire sauce. Shake well.
4. Strain the mixture into the prepared glass.
5. Garnish with a pickle spear, cherry tomatoes, and mini Reuben skewers.

2. Reuben Mary Mimosa:
Ingredients:

- 3 oz champagne
- 1 oz orange juice
- 1 oz tomato juice
- Dash of hot sauce
- Garnish: Mini Reuben sandwich on a skewer

Instructions:

1. In a champagne flute, combine champagne, orange juice, tomato juice, and a dash of hot sauce.
2. Stir gently.
3. Garnish with a mini Reuben sandwich on a skewer.

3. Sauerkraut Spritz:
Ingredients:

- 2 oz gin
- 1 oz elderflower liqueur
- 1 oz sauerkraut juice
- 1/2 oz simple syrup
- Club soda
- Lemon twist (for garnish)

Instructions:

1. In a shaker, combine gin, elderflower liqueur, sauerkraut juice, and simple syrup. Shake well.
2. Strain into a glass filled with ice.
3. Top with club soda.
4. Garnish with a lemon twist.

These Reuben-inspired brunch recipes and cocktails are sure to elevate your brunch experience with a delightful blend of classic flavors and creative twists. In the upcoming chapters, we'll explore Reuben-inspired desserts for a sweet conclusion to your culinary journey.

Chapter 18: Healthy Reuben Alternatives

For those seeking healthier alternatives or accommodating dietary preferences, we'll explore low-carb Reuben options and gluten-free variations. These recipes retain the delicious flavors of a Reuben while providing alternatives for those with specific dietary needs.

Low-Carb Reuben Lettuce Wraps:
Ingredients:

- Large lettuce leaves (such as iceberg or butter lettuce)
- Thinly sliced turkey or chicken breast
- Swiss cheese, sliced
- Sauerkraut
- Russian dressing

Instructions:
Prepare Lettuce Wraps:
Wash and pat dry large lettuce leaves to use as wraps.
Layer Ingredients:
On each lettuce leaf, layer thinly sliced turkey or chicken, Swiss cheese, and sauerkraut.
Drizzle with Dressing:
Drizzle Russian dressing over the ingredients.
Wrap and Serve:
Roll the lettuce leaves to form wraps and secure with toothpicks if needed.

Enjoy these low-carb Reuben lettuce wraps that provide a satisfying and healthy alternative to traditional sandwiches.

Gluten-Free Reuben Casserole:
Ingredients:

- 2 cups cooked quinoa or cauliflower rice
- Thinly sliced corned beef
- Swiss cheese, shredded
- Sauerkraut
- Russian dressing
- Chopped fresh parsley (for garnish)

Instructions:
Preheat Oven:
Preheat your oven to 375°F (190°C).
Layer Ingredients:
In a baking dish, layer cooked quinoa or cauliflower rice, thinly sliced corned beef, sauerkraut, and shredded Swiss cheese.
Drizzle with Dressing:
Drizzle Russian dressing over the layers.
Bake:
Bake in the preheated oven for 15-20 minutes or until the cheese is melted and bubbly.
Garnish and Serve:
Garnish with chopped fresh parsley before serving.
This gluten-free Reuben casserole offers a comforting and nutritious alternative for those with gluten sensitivity or those following a gluten-free diet.

Cauliflower Reuben Bites (Low-Carb and Gluten-Free):
Ingredients:

- Cauliflower florets
- Olive oil
- Smoked paprika
- Garlic powder

- Salt and pepper
- Thinly sliced pastrami or corned beef
- Swiss cheese, sliced
- Sauerkraut
- Russian dressing

Instructions:

Preheat Oven:

Preheat your oven to 425°F (220°C).

Season Cauliflower:

Toss cauliflower florets with olive oil, smoked paprika, garlic powder, salt, and pepper.

Roast Cauliflower:

Spread seasoned cauliflower on a baking sheet and roast for 20-25 minutes or until golden and crisp.

Assemble Bites:

Top each cauliflower bite with a slice of pastrami or corned beef, Swiss cheese, sauerkraut, and a drizzle of Russian dressing.

Broil:

Broil for an additional 2-3 minutes until the cheese is melted and bubbly.

Serve:

Serve these cauliflower Reuben bites as a low-carb and gluten-free appetizer or snack.

These healthy Reuben alternatives provide options for those looking to reduce carbs or avoid gluten while still savoring the iconic flavors of a Reuben.

Chapter 19: Dessert Delights with a Reuben Twist

Elevate your Reuben culinary journey with delightful desserts that carry the essence of this classic sandwich. In this chapter, we'll explore Reuben-inspired desserts and sweet treats that will satisfy the sweet tooth of any Reuben enthusiast.

Rye Chocolate Chip Cookies:

Ingredients:

- 1 cup rye flour
- 1 cup all-purpose flour
- 1/2 teaspoon baking soda
- 1/2 teaspoon salt
- 1/2 cup unsalted butter, softened
- 1/2 cup brown sugar, packed
- 1/2 cup granulated sugar
- 1 large egg
- 1 teaspoon vanilla extract
- 1 cup chocolate chips

Instructions:

Preheat Oven:

Preheat your oven to 350°F (175°C) and line a baking sheet with parchment paper.

Mix Dry Ingredients:

In a bowl, whisk together rye flour, all-purpose flour, baking soda, and salt.

Cream Butter and Sugars:

In a separate bowl, cream together softened butter, brown sugar, and granulated sugar until light and fluffy.

Add Egg and Vanilla:

Add the egg and vanilla extract to the creamed butter and sugar. Mix until well combined.

Combine Wet and Dry Mixtures:

Gradually add the dry ingredients to the wet ingredients, mixing until just combined.

Fold in Chocolate Chips:

Gently fold in the chocolate chips.

Bake:

Drop rounded tablespoons of dough onto the prepared baking sheet.

Bake for 10-12 minutes or until the edges are golden.

Cool and Enjoy:

Allow the cookies to cool on the baking sheet for a few minutes before transferring them to a wire rack to cool completely.

These Rye Chocolate Chip Cookies offer a subtle twist with the addition of rye flour, providing a unique and delicious Reuben-inspired treat.

Russian Dressing Cheesecake Bars:

Ingredients:

For the Crust:

- 1 1/2 cups graham cracker crumbs
- 1/2 cup unsalted butter, melted
- 1/4 cup sugar

For the Cheesecake Filling:

- 3 packages (8 oz each) cream cheese, softened
- 1 cup sugar
- 3 large eggs

- 1 teaspoon vanilla extract
- 1/2 cup sour cream

For the Russian Dressing Swirl:

- 1/4 cup Russian dressing

Instructions:
Preheat Oven:
Preheat your oven to 325°F (163°C) and line a baking pan with parchment paper, leaving an overhang on the sides.
Make Crust:
In a bowl, combine graham cracker crumbs, melted butter, and sugar. Press the mixture into the bottom of the prepared pan.

Prepare Cheesecake Filling:

- In a large mixing bowl, beat cream cheese and sugar until smooth.
- Add eggs, one at a time, beating well after each addition.
- Mix in vanilla extract and sour cream until fully combined.

Assemble Cheesecake Bars:
Pour the cream cheese mixture over the crust in the pan.
Add Russian Dressing Swirl:
Drizzle Russian dressing over the cream cheese mixture. Use a knife or toothpick to create a swirl pattern.
Bake:
Bake for 35-40 minutes or until the center is set.
Chill and Slice:

- Allow the cheesecake bars to cool in the pan, then refrigerate for at least 4 hours or overnight.

- Once chilled, use the parchment paper overhang to lift the bars from the pan and slice into squares.

These Russian Dressing Cheesecake Bars offer a playful and unexpected twist with the incorporation of the iconic dressing into a sweet treat.

Dark Chocolate Sauerkraut Cupcakes:

Ingredients:

For the Cupcakes:

- 1 cup all-purpose flour
- 1/2 cup unsweetened cocoa powder
- 1 teaspoon baking powder
- 1/2 teaspoon baking soda
- 1/4 teaspoon salt
- 1/2 cup unsalted butter, softened
- 1 cup sugar
- 2 large eggs
- 1 teaspoon vanilla extract
- 1/2 cup buttermilk
- 1/2 cup sauerkraut, drained and finely chopped

For the Frosting:

- 8 oz dark chocolate, chopped
- 1 cup heavy cream
- 1/4 cup powdered sugar
- 1 teaspoon vanilla extract

Instructions:

Preheat Oven:

Preheat your oven to 350°F (175°C) and line a muffin tin with cupcake liners.

Mix Dry Ingredients:

In a bowl, whisk together flour, cocoa powder, baking powder, baking soda, and salt.

Cream Butter and Sugar:

In another bowl, cream together softened butter and sugar until light and fluffy.

Add Eggs and Vanilla:

Add eggs, one at a time, beating well after each addition. Mix in vanilla extract.

Combine Wet and Dry Mixtures:

Gradually add the dry ingredients to the wet ingredients, alternating with buttermilk. Begin and end with the dry ingredients.

Fold in Sauerkraut:

Gently fold in the chopped sauerkraut.

Fill Cupcake Liners:

Divide the batter among the cupcake liners, filling each about two-thirds full.

Bake:

Bake for 18-20 minutes or until a toothpick inserted into the center comes out clean.

Make Chocolate Ganache Frosting:

While the cupcakes are cooling, make the chocolate ganache by heating the heavy cream until just simmering and pouring it over the chopped dark chocolate. Let it sit for a minute, then stir until smooth. Stir in powdered sugar and vanilla extract.

Frost Cupcakes:

Once the cupcakes are completely cooled, frost them with the dark chocolate ganache.

These Dark Chocolate Sauerkraut Cupcakes offer a rich and moist chocolate base with a surprising twist of sauerkraut, creating a unique and delightful dessert.

These Reuben-inspired desserts and sweet treats add a sweet conclusion to your culinary journey. Whether you're a Reuben enthusiast or someone looking to explore new and creative flavors, these desserts are sure to leave a lasting impression.

Embarking on this culinary journey through the world of Reuben-inspired recipes has been a delightful exploration of flavors, creativity, and culinary innovation. From mastering the basics of the classic Reuben to crafting unique variations, sides, snacks, dips, spreads, and even venturing into the realm of brunch, we've covered a vast array of delicious dishes.

The journey didn't stop with savory delights; we also delved into the sweet side of things, bringing you desserts that carry the essence of the iconic Reuben sandwich. Rye Chocolate Chip Cookies, Russian Dressing Cheesecake Bars, and Dark Chocolate Sauerkraut Cupcakes added a sweet and unexpected twist to the traditional flavors.

Whether you're a seasoned cook or an adventurous beginner, these recipes offer a mix of classic comfort and creative inspiration. The Reuben sandwich, with its layers of corned beef, Swiss cheese, sauerkraut, and Russian dressing, served as the muse for countless culinary adventures.

Remember, these recipes are merely a starting point. Feel free to adapt and personalize them to suit your taste preferences and dietary needs. Cooking is an art, and each dish is a canvas for your creativity.

As you savor these Reuben-inspired creations, may they bring joy to your table, spark lively conversations, and create lasting memories. Whether shared with friends and family or savored in solitude, these dishes carry the spirit of culinary exploration and the joy of discovering new and delightful flavors.

Thank you for joining me on this flavorful journey. If you ever find yourself craving more culinary adventures or have specific tastes you'd like to explore, I'm here to guide you. Happy cooking and bon appétit!